GREAT ANIMAL COMEBACKS

SAVING THE AMERICAN BISON

by Karen Latchana Kenney

pogo

Ideas for Parents and Teachers

Pogo Books let children practice reading informational text while introducing them to nonfiction features such as headings, labels, sidebars, maps, and diagrams, as well as a table of contents, glossary, and index.

Carefully leveled text with a strong photo match offers early fluent readers the support they need to succeed.

Before Reading

- "Walk" through the book and point out the various nonfiction features. Ask the student what purpose each feature serves.
- Look at the glossary together. Read and discuss the words.

Read the Book

- Have the child read the book independently.
- Invite him or her to list questions that arise from reading.

After Reading

- Discuss the child's questions. Talk about how he or she might find answers to those questions.
- Prompt the child to think more. Ask: Have you ever seen an American bison? Where was it? Were you surprised by its size?

Pogo Books are published by Jump!
5357 Penn Avenue South
Minneapolis, MN 55419
www.jumplibrary.com

Copyright © 2019 Jump!
International copyright reserved in all countries.
No part of this book may be reproduced in any form without written permission from the publisher.

Library of Congress Cataloging-in-Publication Data

Names: Kenney, Karen Latchana, author.
Title: Saving the American bison /
by Karen Latchana Kenney.
Description: Pogo books edition. | Minneapolis, MN: Jump!, Inc., [2019]
Series: Great animal comebacks | Audience: Age 7-10.
Includes index.
Identifiers: LCCN 2018024905 (print)
LCCN 2018027527 (ebook)
ISBN 9781641282796 (ebook)
ISBN 9781641282789 (hardcover : alk. paper)
Subjects: LCSH: American bison—Conservation—Juvenile literature.
Classification: LCC QL737.U53 (ebook) | LCC QL737.U53 K46 2019 (print) | DDC 599.64/3—dc23
LC record available at https://lccn.loc.gov/2018024905

Editor: Jenna Trnka
Designer: Anna Peterson

Photo Credits: CarbonBrain/iStock, cover; Eric Isselee/Shutterstock, 1, 23; karenfoleyphotography/iStock, 3; Images by Dr. Alan Lipkin/Shutterstock, 4; KGrif/iStock, 5; LaserLens/iStock, 6-7; Underwood Archives/Getty, 8-9; Science History Images/Alamy, 10; Humphrey Dunn/Getty, 11; Kelly Vandellen/Dreamstime, 12-13 (foreground); Theron Stripling III/Shutterstock, 12-13 (background); Jim Brandenburg/Minden Pictures/SuperStock, 14-15; Carl M Christensen/Getty, 16; Whidbey Panoramas/Alamy, 17; Martin Castrogiovanni/Shutterstock, 18-19; Rich Reid/Getty, 20-21.

Printed in the United States of America at Corporate Graphics in North Mankato, Minnesota.

TABLE OF CONTENTS

CHAPTER 1

AN ANIMAL IN DANGER

A large **mammal** grazes. It chews on grass. This is the American bison.

It is not alone. This is Yellowstone **National Park**. Close to 5,000 live here! But wild bison were once hard to find. Why? They almost went **extinct**.

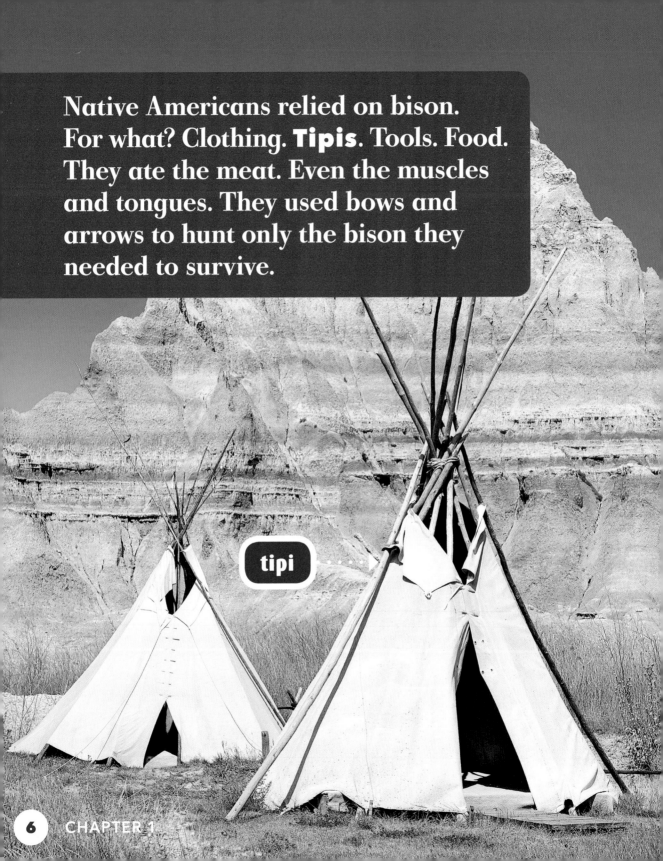

Native Americans relied on bison. For what? Clothing. **Tipis**. Tools. Food. They ate the meat. Even the muscles and tongues. They used bows and arrows to hunt only the bison they needed to survive.

tipi

TAKE A LOOK!

Native Americans used every part of the bison. For what? Take a look at some of the uses.

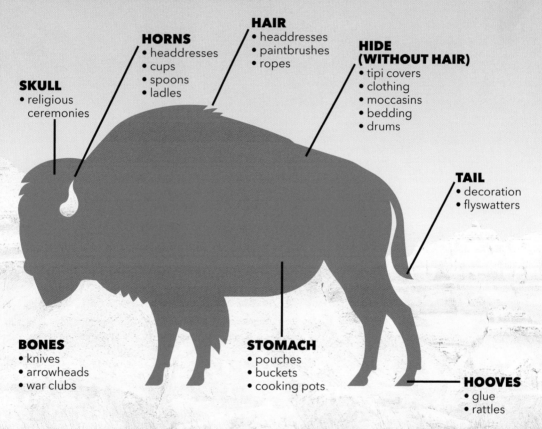

HAIR
• headdresses
• paintbrushes
• ropes

HORNS
• headdresses
• cups
• spoons
• ladles

HIDE (WITHOUT HAIR)
• tipi covers
• clothing
• moccasins
• bedding
• drums

SKULL
• religious ceremonies

TAIL
• decoration
• flyswatters

BONES
• knives
• arrowheads
• war clubs

STOMACH
• pouches
• buckets
• cooking pots

HOOVES
• glue
• rattles

bison skins

White settlers killed many bison in the early 1800s. Sometimes just for sport. Other times they sold the **hides** and bones.

The railroad brought more people to the West. They shot bison from trains. Bison **herds** began disappearing.

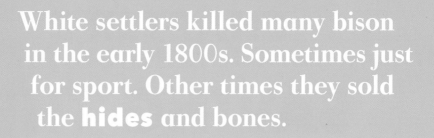

DID YOU KNOW?

Bison once ruled the **Great Plains**. There were believed to be between 30 and 60 million!

CHAPTER 2

· ·

SAVING THE BISON

William T. Hornaday was a **zoologist**. He wanted to find out how many bison were left. He wrote to people around the country. They wrote back with their counts.

· · · · · **William T. Hornaday**

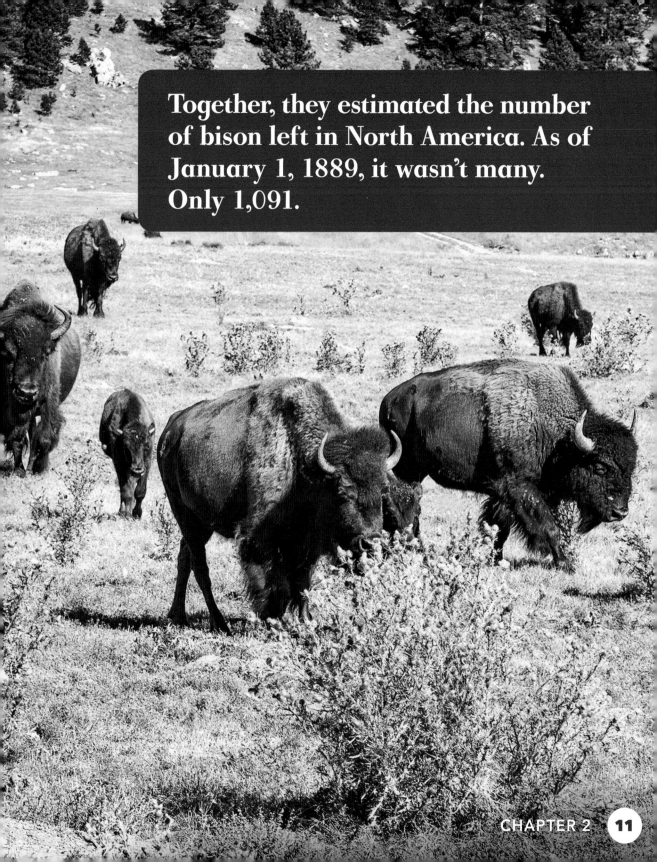

Together, they estimated the number of bison left in North America. As of January 1, 1889, it wasn't many. Only 1,091.

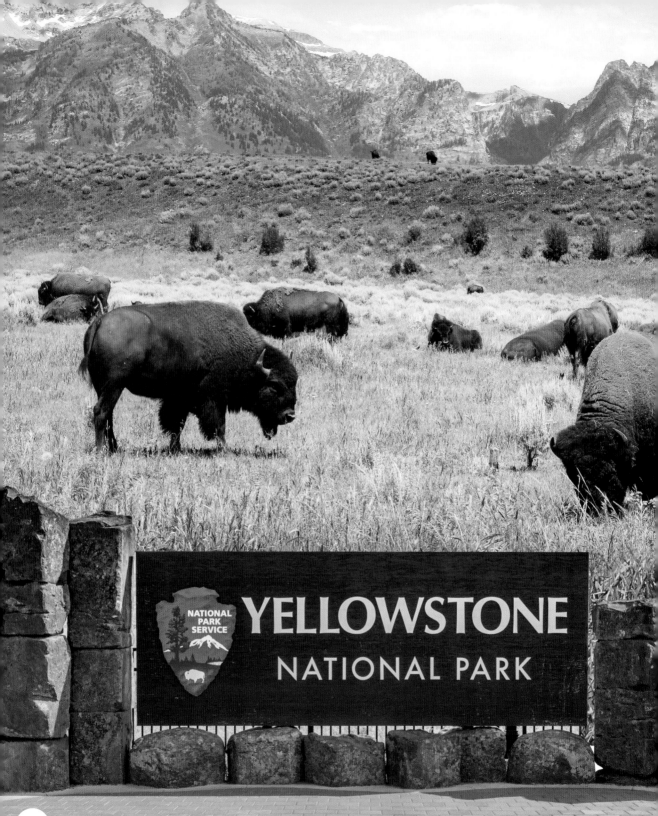

Where were they? One place
was Yellowstone National Park.
In 1894, a law passed.
It protected animals here.
No one could hunt them.

Hornaday helped form the American Bison Society. When? In 1905. It asked the government to protect more bison. Where? On **reserves**.

The first herd was only 15 bison. It was sent to Oklahoma. How? By train. They went to Wichita National Forest. The society placed herds in more national parks. The government started more herds.

bison reserve

CHAPTER 3

BISON TODAY

Today, bison roam **prairies** and mountains. They are safe in national parks. In state parks. And on reserves. People can only hunt them with **permits**. Parks issue very few permits each year. This keeps herds at a good size.

bison farm

Bison also live on ranches and farms. People can pay to hunt bison on ranches. Farmers raise bison for their meat. Some Native American tribes have herds, too.

One place to see bison is Custer State Park. It is in the Black Hills of South Dakota.

Close to 1,300 bison live here. Each year, people ride on horses and gather the herd. Bison **stampede** across the plains. It sounds like thunder. The ground shakes.

DID YOU KNOW?

Bison are the largest land mammals in North America. How big? Males can weigh 2,000 pounds (907 kilograms) or more!

Bison herds continue to grow. More than 500,000 bison are alive today.

We almost lost bison forever. But we saved them just in time. Would you like to see them?

DID YOU KNOW?

Bison are a **keystone species**. They eat many grasses. They make room for new plants to grow. This keeps plains healthy.

ACTIVITIES & TOOLS

BE A ZOOLOGIST

Practice being a zoologist like William T. Hornaday and conduct your own observations of animals around you!

What You Need:
- notebook
- pencil
- binoculars (optional)
- camera (optional)

❶ Pick a species in your area to observe.

❷ Observe the animal's behavior. What does it eat? Does it make any noises? If the animal is faraway, use binoculars to watch.

❸ Write down your findings. If you want, take pictures to help you document your findings.

❹ Observe the animal every day for a week. What do you notice that is the same each day? What is different?

❺ Can you count the number of animals you see each day? Record all of your findings. What does it tell you about the species?

GLOSSARY

extinct: No longer found alive.

Great Plains: A large region of plains that spans from Canada into Texas through the west central United States.

herds: Large groups of animals that live and move together.

hides: The skins of animals.

keystone species: A species of plant or animal that has a major impact on and is essential to the ecosystem in which it belongs.

mammal: A warm-blooded animal that has hair and gives birth to live young.

national park: A large section of land that is protected by the federal government for people to visit and to preserve wildlife.

permits: Official documents that give people permission to do something.

prairies: Large, flat areas of land with rolling grassland and few or no trees.

reserves: Protected places where hunting is not allowed and animals can live and breed safely.

stampede: To make a sudden, wild rush in one direction.

tipis: Cone-shaped tents made from animal skins.

zoologist: A scientist who studies animals.

INDEX

TO LEARN MORE

Finding more information is as easy as 1, 2, 3.

① **Go to www.factsurfer.com**

② **Enter "savingtheAmericanbison" into the search box.**

③ **Click the "Surf" button to see a list of websites.**

FACT SURFER